MW00611743

MEMORIES FROM A

Hill Country

GARDEN

MEMORIES FROM A

Hill Country

GARDEN

Flowers, Stones, and Critters

Jim Truchard

GREENLEAF
BOOK GROUP PRESS

Published by Greenleaf Book Group Press
Austin, Texas
www.gbgpress.com

Copyright ©2013 James Truchard
All rights reserved.

No part of this book may be reproduced, stored in a retrieval system, or transmitted by any means, electronic, mechanical, photocopying, recording, or otherwise, without written permission from the copyright holder.

Design and composition by Greenleaf Book Group LLC
Cover design by Greenleaf Book Group LLC
All photos by Jim Truchard

Publisher's Cataloging-In-Publication Data
Truchard, Jim.
  Memories from a Hill Country garden : flowers, stones, and critters / Jim Truchard.—1st ed.
  p. : chiefly col. ill. ; cm.

  Includes index.
  ISBN: 978-1-60832-580-1

  1. Natural history—Texas—Texas Hill Country—Pictorial works. 2. Gardens—Texas—Texas Hill Country—Pictorial works. 3. Plants--Texas—Texas Hill Country—Pictorial works. 4. Insects—Texa—Texas Hill Country—Pictorial works. 5. Animals—Texas—Texas Hill Country—Pictorial works. I. Title.

QH105.T4 T78 2014
508.764   2013944430

Part of the Tree Neutral® program, which offsets the number of trees consumed in the production and printing of this book by taking proactive steps, such as planting trees in direct proportion to the number of trees used: www.treeneutral.com

TreeNeutral®

Printed by Imago in China on acid-free paper

13 14 15 16 17 18   10 9 8 7 6 5 4 3 2 1

First Edition

This book is dedicated to my wife, Lee, who shared countless hours with me enjoying our Hill Country garden. Each season of pictures is a memory book of our time together that I will never forget.

Preface

This book is intended to be a tribute to the unique character of the Texas Hill Country. I can only hope to capture a part of the land's charm I have known for the last fifty years. My appreciation of the Hill Country started with a geology course at the University of Texas at Austin. I learned about the Balcones fault that uplifted the land west of Austin some millions of years ago and the subsequent erosion that shaped and carved the terrain of the Hill Country. When I graduated from the University with my PhD, the lure of the Hill Country was strong and I was motivated to found a company in Austin.

The photographs from my garden span fourteen years. With time, the garden became a private sanctuary for my wife, Lee, and myself where we enjoyed a high level of privacy along with the birds and animals. Each year the number of mockingbirds, red birds, and doves has increased, making an even more delightful setting. That, along with the wild terrain immediately below the garden, has provided a home for squirrels, possums, raccoons, and a den of foxes.

It's change that makes a garden enticing. Each day finds new flowers, each season a new mood, and each year a new start.

Like much of the Hill Country, the lot that became our garden began with some bare rocks and a few oak trees. After many truckloads of soil and compost, a rich garden was established. Indigenous native plants were planted first, followed by plants native to Texas, Mexico, and elsewhere in the United States. Finally, hardy plants from the rest of the world were used for their special ability to withstand Hill Country summers and winters. Birds and squirrels introduced additional plants from neighboring gardens and from the lake area below, creating some randomness to the garden order.

This book is organized by seasons starting with summer, a season often regarded by many non–Hill Country residents as being too harsh to support a compelling garden. As you will see, a wide variety of plants not only survive, but thrive, in the Hill Country's hot and humid climate. I have provided detailed descriptions for some of the more unique plants along with some of my personal experiences with the varied growing conditions, such as climate and soil conditions.

One unique charm of the Hill Country is the natural stone that has been sculpted over thousands of years. Stone creates the frame for the garden and brings the Hill Country character alive. I personally chose and placed many of the smaller stones. Stones create permanence as the years and seasons come and go. As Willie Nelson put it, "Nothing lasts forever but old Fords and natural stone."

As camera technology changed, so did my photography. The first pictures were taken with a point-and-shoot 35mm film camera. Later pictures were taken with digital cameras starting with five megapixels and progressing to two twenty-four-megapixel cameras with high-quality lenses. Most pictures were taken in either the morning or in the evening, some with overcast skies. In some cases, especially with red flowers, I would time picture taking with the light of the setting sun. I used a flash at times to capture the wings of a hummingbird or simply to provide some fill-in light.

Lee and I spent many evenings in the front yard entertained by hummingbirds, mockingbirds, redbirds, and squirrels. Southern breezes and evening shade made even summer evenings comfortable. Once the sun was close to setting, we would retire to our upper deck to observe an often-spectacular Hill Country sunset.

The book opens with a description of some of the elements that make the Hill Country unique, including a sunrise with its distinct light for photography. The book closes with a special sunset dedicated to my wife, Lee. I attempted to capture the mood of the seasons and the role they play in shaping the character of the Hill Country.

Texas sunrise

Earth's Elements in the Garden

Sun

Along with soil and water, sunlight is a major ingredient in Hill Country gardening success. Some plants, like 'Texas Star' hibiscus and okra, demand full sun and high temperatures to thrive. Most herbs also enjoy full sun.

When planning a garden, you must consider the shade conditions of your landscape. In planting trees and shrubs, consider the shade that will eventually cover the surrounding terrain when plants mature. Over the last fourteen years some of the sunny spots in my garden have become shaded. Some species will no longer thrive once their locations receive less direct sun.

Many plants like limited hours of sunlight, and grow best in dappled or full shade. Some are versatile, thriving among a variety of light conditions. Others will grow in partial shade but bloom only lightly. Columbines, red mountain sage, and many pepper varieties seem to have favorite spots. Some experimentation is often needed to find that perfect spot. Generally, morning sun and evening shade is best for these. Plants like red mountain sage bloom when days shorten.

Lighting conditions matter for photography as well. Early morning offers excellent light. Likewise, cloud cover offers a lot of flexibility for shadow-free pictures. Evening light with its red cast is preferred for certain scenes. The full sun of midday offers maximum light for special cases, like maximum depth of field shots or telephoto shots. Of course, sunrises and sunsets create their own display of color to be captured on film.

Rain

According to experts, the average Hill Country rainfall is around thirty-two inches per year. But the annual average does not tell the whole story, as rainfall is very unevenly distributed throughout the year. The Hill Country is known for flash floods with as much as a foot of rain falling over a short period of time. Generally, summer rains arrive as thunderstorms separated by weeks of hot, dry weather. Fall brings fronts that often produce rain. Winter brings slow rains. Spring showers water the flowers that make the Hill Country famous. In addition to rainfall, my garden is watered by three sources: stored rainwater, lake water, and house water. My rainwater tank is a 36,000-gallon ferrocement elliptical tank 36'×19' that stands ten feet high.

The Soil

The rich blackland soil in the Hill Country is the result of the limestone weathering process and contains organic material from an ancient sea. It's well known that blackland soil, with its carbon and minerals, offers a more fertile starting point than sandy soil. I find value in the alluvial deposits of black soil found throughout the Hill Country. However, gardeners aren't always so lucky to find this element in their land, and Hill Country soil often needs special attention to make it a viable growing material.

Some soil has high clay content; dense and gummy when wet and hard and laced with cracks when dry. Other is caliche, or marl, often found on natural slopes. Amazingly, some natives such as gayfeather and mountain pink thrive in this soil.

My lot started with little tillable soil. Only after the addition of four thousand cubic yards of soil and three hundred cubic yards of compost was there deep enough soil for a garden. A city requirement that all rainwater drain to the street complicated landscaping. The installation of a 36,000-gallon rainwater system helped. Overflow from this tank flows to the street.

Plants with wetter feet were planted in areas with less drainage. The cactus area was created with a three-way mix of soil, sand, and compost. The formal garden area has soil that is a combination of granite sand, soil, and compost. Overall about half the soil was purchased and half was brought in from excavation sites. In general the free soil was of higher quality, as some purchased soil had high concentrations of alkaline clay.

Compost

Compost is one of nature's wonders. It is black gold for any garden. It's amazing stuff. You start with every weed, leaf, clipping, or kitchen waste, add a little water and air, and presto! It works like magic to feed plants and help them to thrive.

My garden actually produces more compost than I can use, so I share it with friends. Instead of turning the compost, I use an air pump and a pipe to force air into the pile. The right amount of air and water is important for speedy composting. Be careful when trying to add nitrogen with commercial fertilizer as it may contain weed killer; a gardening pro will use manure to help boost the compost.

One downside of my compost pile is that not all seeds are killed before they are mixed in. This means extra weeding in areas where the compost is spread.

Before introducing the compost to the garden, be sure it is ready, because compost will deplete oxygen from the soil if it is not. I use an annual cycle, building one pile while using the other to ensure I always have ready compost.

Stones

No symbol of the Hill Country is more important than the stone. Limestone formed here some sixty-five million years ago during the cretaceous age and shapes the character of the region. In fact, the Balcones fault that uplifted the stone some twenty-five million years ago defines the eastern boundary of the Hill Country. The wide variety of limestone formations add to the mystique of Hill Country stone.

Water, nature's sculptor, has created many shapes and art forms. My "collection" was selected from a combination of stone yards, construction sites, generous neighbors, and stones found on the original lot. The large stacked walls were built with stone that was excavated onsite. Dry-stacked flat stone walls have demonstrated their ability to last hundreds if not thousands of years. While many Hill Country retaining walls are built with small stones from limestone quarries, my walls were built with stones weighing up to a quarter- to a half-ton. Dry stacked stone walls offer an excellent way to create tiered levels that resemble naturally occurring cliffs.

The stone ledge, mined onsite from boulders for retaining walls, also forms the rock deck upon which the fire pit and stone table are placed. The fire pit's stone seats were selected from our corporate construction site and the onsite excavation. The retaining wall adjacent the pool is constructed from stone selected from a quarry site. Selections of this stone were also used for a stone table, reminiscent of one in the Flintstone cartoons.

Spaces between the stones offer harbor for many plants that require excellent drainage. These include blackfoot daisies, white mistflower, and gayfeather. Ferns enjoy a little extra winter protection from heat stored in the stones. Puddles that form on the surface of large stones create welcome birdbaths. Some of my favorite stones are honeycomb, stones with large holes etched by water over many years. Of course I have a soft spot for the gray smooth stones as well. The unique shape of each could be considered nature's artwork.

Maya

Maya enjoyed the stones, as they provided walking pathways and sitting perches. Maya chased the rock squirrels that made their home in the crevices between the stones. Unfortunately for Maya, a skunk family would occasionally take residence in the stone wall. Fortunately there's an excellent recipe with hydrogen peroxide that helps to remove skunk odor from a dog's coat. Squirrels, foxes and other animals also used the stone walls as pathways.

Texas Persimmon

Summer

Along with Hill Country winters, summer also defines what is possible in a Hill Country garden. Hill Country summers have a reputation for being too hostile to create a luscious garden. Fortunately, there are options that make it possible to keep the blooms coming. Flowers that excel in hot weather are showing their "Texas-tough" stuff. Some of the toughest, like big red sage, turk's cap, and flame acanthus, are favorites of resident hummingbirds. Members of the hibiscus family reach their prime as daily temperatures rise. Unfortunately, some of these summer heroes miss the spring and fall garden shows.

Summer is prime time for long-blooming favorites like lantanas, purple coneflowers, and water lilies. Hardy imports are important options for flowering trees. Two of the best are crepe myrtle and purple chaste tree, or Vitex. Summer flowers attract butterflies that seem oblivious to high temperatures. Native birds are busy raising their families. Ripening flower seeds and anacua berries provide food for birds and animals, like squirrels, foxes, raccoons, and unfortunately an occasional skunk. By mid-June, daily temperatures are rising and spring rains have stopped. Only an occasional shower will interrupt the dry Hill Country summer. Some summers, I use up my stored rainwater by mid-August. In 2011 the severe drought wreaked havoc on gardens and wild trees alike. Many native trees died in the wild and dry forests, culminating in very destructive wild fires.

High temperatures coupled with high humidity create a challenge for plants that have low tolerance for these conditions. Notable examples are lavender, 'Nuevo Leon' autumn sage, and garden sage. Roses that were splendid in the spring now have wilted blooms.

Hummingbirds and other wildlife adjust to high temperatures by feeding early in the morning and late in the afternoon. Likewise, humans must adjust to adapt to summer's high temperatures. Special attention to the shade and summer breezes is important. This means planning outdoor time for the early morning and late afternoon. I have a few favorite spots to relax in my garden. One is to sit on the shady loop of the driveway that runs next to the pond. Another is the upper deck. Strategically placed on the side of the house, the deck offers a breezy respite from the summer heat as the sun sets.

Butterfly Bush, White

Big Red Sage

Big red sage, a native of the Hill Country, still has limited availability and was once thought to be extinct. It is a rare plant in nature, found only in the Edwards Plateau. It is important not to collect seed from wild populations. Only obtain Big red sage seed or plants from a reputable grower. Big red sage is a favorite of hummingbirds. A hummingbird will visit every bloom five or more times a day, guarding the flower from other hummingbirds. Big red sage is a summer bloomer, so it misses the spring and fall garden shows.

Big red sage is a perennial and will reseed. Like most sages, it's trouble-free. It grows in relatively dry soil as well as relatively wet soil, but most enjoys a well-drained spot among limestone boulders.

Hummingbirds

No Hill Country garden would be complete without hummingbirds. There are hummingbird residents that make my garden their home and then there are migrants, just passing through on their way to and from Mexico. Many of the native flowers are favorites, with big red sage and Turk's cap topping the list. A hummingbird will pick a flower and guard it jealously. A nearby twig provides a convenient perch from which to launch an attack on an intruding hummingbird. Sentinel duty can consume hours. Meanwhile, honeybees are making off with all the pollen. The first northers bring the migrants, typically around the middle of September. Often more aggressive than the residents, the migrants take over the best flowers. Hummingbirds are the most determined feeders just before dusk, an excellent time to take photographs or just be entertained by their antics. A long bill and even longer tongue help them with trumpet-shaped flowers such as salvias, esperanza, and flame acanthus.

Hill Country Sunflowers

Sunflowers adorn the fields across the Texas Hill Country. These sunflowers are a major food source for birds, especially goldfinches, sparrows, and sometimes redbirds. The sunflower readily reseeds and is a vigorous grower in cultivated soil. The University of Texas Law School has a tradition of using the Hill Country sunflower as part of its graduation ceremony.

Scarlet Sage

Salvia coccinea (scarlet sage) is a showy southern native that grows in sandy soils. Since it grows widely across the Americas, there is quite a bit of variation in its growing and blooming habits among the cultivars. The native variety grows in sandy soils, in thickets, in open woods, and edges in east and south Texas. My scarlet sage has survived many winters, especially in protected locations. There has been quite a bit of variation in how prolific each cultivar blooms, depending on the amount of shade.

'Texas Star' Hibiscus

'Texas Star' hibiscus is a true star in a Texas garden, with new blooms every day during the Texas summer. Plucked flowers last for a day without needing to be put in water. 'Texas Star' likes full sun and a moist to wet spot to grow. 'Texas Star' starts blooming just as summer heat turns on. It continues to bloom throughout the summer, giving welcome color when it's needed most.

Purple Chaste Tree (Vitex)

Like crepe myrtles, vitex is a native of China but has adapted to the Hill Country very well. It's like the bumper sticker that reads, "I wasn't born in Texas, but I got here as fast as I could." Mine are purple-blue, but shades vary from white to blue. Vitex is a profuse bloomer starting in early summer with intermittent blooms until early fall. The upright, spike-like flowers grow on the tips of new growth. The flowers are favorites of butterflies, bees, and hummingbirds. Vitex can be a small shrub or small spreading tree up to twenty-five feet. They are extremely hardy and can be found growing near old homes, farms, or cemeteries. Vitex has no major insect or disease problems. Vitex has a pleasant spicy fragrance both in the flowers and the leaves. Vitex is often called purple chaste tree due to the reputed belief that the seeds "subdue the sexual urge." Purple chaste tree can become an invader on the banks of rivers and lakes so please avoid planting it near those areas.

Autumn Sage

Autumn sage is a native of southwest Texas and northern Mexico. Despite its name, autumn sage blooms throughout the summer and autumn until cooler weather sets in. A wide variety of colors are available from nurseries, including rose, white, pink, orange, lavender, violet, and red. I have grown white, coral, orange, violet, and red. Autumn sage is hardy and grows well in shady spots such as an eastern or northeastern exposure in an area with excellent drainage with a half-day or full day of sun. No Hill Country garden would be complete without autumn sage. Once established, this hardy perennial requires little maintenance, except to trim it in mid-February.

Bourgainvillea

The Nine-Banded Armadillo

Next to the bluebonnet, the armadillo is one of the most widely recognized symbols for Texas. In 1981 the armadillo was designated the official state mascot. The armadillo is a relative newcomer to the Hill Country, having arrived around the end of the nineteenth century.

Armadillos have few natural enemies; however, they are well known as roadkill because of their habit of jumping up to bumper height of an approaching car.

Some gardeners regard armadillos as a nuisance, as they dig holes in flowerbeds and the lawn in their search for insects, grubs, and spiders, and unfortunately an occasional earthworm. Females bear identical quadruplets. Armadillos are known to carry leprosy, a disease brought to the Americas by Europeans.

Chives

I started with a few chive plants and now have chives growing throughout the garden. Chives reseed readily and divide by their bulbs. I have given away many chive plants. I now cut the bloom stems after they bloom. Chives are an excellent garden herb to use as a garnish for baked potatoes, an ingredient in salad dressings, and even as a starting point for roux in Cajun food, as my chives resemble the special onions often used to make roux. Chive blooms are a favorite of bees.

Buffalo Bur

Buffalo Bur is found on dry, rocky soils and disturbed areas. Minute hairs cover the stems and leaves, which are defended by numerous yellow prickles. The fruit is a capsule, also protected by yellow prickles.

Bumblebees

Bumblebees are important pollinators of native flowers and food crops such as blueberries, squash, watermelons, and tomatoes. Texas has nine species of bumblebees, identified by their thorax pattern. As a child I was very frightened by the presence of a bumblebee, perhaps because of their large size. I now know that unless you try to catch one in your hand or step on a nest, they are usually harmless.

Crepe Myrtles

Crepe myrtles provide summer color. We have China to thank for this Texas-tough import. Crepe myrtles are one of only a few flowering shrubs and trees with a long blooming season. They vary in size from a small shrub to thirty-feet-tall, multi-trunk trees. It's important to pick the right size for the location. Colors vary from white to deep red with many shades in between. Crepe myrtle leaves add fall color, while its unique bark adds color in the winter. We love our natives, but sometimes we have to think global for a Texas-hardy garden. Crepe myrtles transplant easily during the dormant season. Many of mine were seedlings that were transplanted.

Desert Honeysuckle

Desert Willow

Every Hill Country garden can find a spot for a desert willow. Desert willow is a hardy native Texas tree with a light wispy canopy. This medium-sized tree blooms all summer. Blooms range from light pink to burgundy. Like its cousin, desert trumpet vine, it has a trumpet-shaped bloom that appears in clusters. Desert willow is not a willow at all. Its relatives include crossvine and catalpa. It is native across the southwestern United States, including southwest Texas. Desert willow is a drought-tolerant, deciduous tree that grows fifteen- to twenty-five-feet-tall.

41

Dragonfly

Dragonflies have been adored since ancient times and still provide enchantment to a modern garden. Dragonflies are living fossils that predate dinosaurs. As one of our good insects, dragonflies neither sting nor bite humans, and they eat large quantities of gnats, flies, and mosquitoes. As a matter of fact, one memorable evening a large swarm of gnats was disturbing the peace on our upper deck when a swarm of dragonflies came up and ate every one. Thank heaven for prehistoric monsters! Although dragonflies love to stay near a pond, they will range some distance for food. They love a high perch such as a fence post, a stick, or an upright branch where they can scan the sky with their very large eyes that see in all directions.

Orange Dragonfly

Flame Acanthus

Figs

Flame Acanthus

Flame acanthus is one of the top attractors of hummingbirds. It is covered with slender orange blooms from midsummer to frost. Flame acanthus is a drought-tolerant, heat-loving plant that grows in well-drained soil, even in my cactus garden. Flame acanthus is a native of west and south-central Texas where it grows on rocky banks and flood plains. This orange flower blooms throughout the Texas Longhorn football season.

43

Frog Fruit

Frogs

44

Currant Tomato

Currant tomatoes are the ultimate heirloom tomato. Obvious differentiaters for this tomato are its size (it's only about ⅓-inch in diameter) and that it is not self-pollinated. This tomato is bursting with flavor. This very sweet tomato has significantly more lycopene than common tomatoes, making it a healthy addition to a vegetable garden. Currant tomatoes are a delightful addition to a salad. I also enjoy eating them straight off the vine. These tomatoes grow in clusters spaced a foot or more apart; as such, they take a lot of space, with vines growing ten feet or more. The plants are extremely hardy and will produce throughout the summer, but they are susceptible to root knot. Currant tomatoes readily reseed in the garden. I just move them to a new location if necessary. Since my original purchase, I've never had to plant seeds. These tiny gems are ideal for a children's garden.

Damselflies are the smaller cousins of dragonflies. Unlike dragonflies, damselflies have wings that are folded together above their back when perched.

Jimson Weed

It could be said that jimson weed has a bloom too soft and tender to thrive in the Hill Country, but thrive it does. Jimson weed is a member of the nightshade family; as such it is very poisonous. Its large, bright white blooms open at night and close as soon as sunlight strikes them. Bees rush out at dawn to harvest the pollen. Jimson weed is sometimes called "thorn apple" because of its globular, poisonous seedpods.

Lantana

Lantana comes in many sizes and colors. My favorite is the orange and yellow lantana native to the Texas Hill Country. Mockingbirds love the berries and propagate the seeds widely. The pink and yellow native of Bermuda seems to be the most prolific. Lantanas are transplanted easily in the winter and are one of our most durable hot-summer bloomers.

Lemon Balm

Lemon balm is a Texas-tough herb. It has few pests and is very hardy, even in the heat of summer. It is a strong antioxidant and features a long list of attributed health benefits, including treating melancholy, antiviral and antibacterial properties, improving mental performance, moderating Alzheimer symptoms, serving as a mosquito repellant, and treating of hyperthyroidism.

I use lemon balm to make my favorite herbal tea. I really don't understand why it's not more widely grown, considering its many alleged benefits. To make lemon balm tea I fill up a one-gallon pitcher with leaves (fresh-grown tips are best), add water, and heat in the microwave for ten minutes. Amazingly, the leaves can be reused for several weeks. Lemon balm tea is welcome on a hot summer day—especially with ice and vodka. Lemon balm prefers a sunny spot and will spread with runners, but it is not as aggressive as typical mints. It also readily reseeds and can be invasive if not trimmed after blooming. Leaves can be harvested from spring until the first hard freeze.

Lemon Balm

Mexican Honeysuckle

Mexican honeysuckle is a must for a hummingbird garden. Its bright orange flowers not only attract hummingbirds but also Texas Longhorn fans. This native of Mexico is a small shrub that isn't fussy and blooms most of the year. This plant is fairly drought tolerant and grows in light shade to full sun.

Mexican Honeysuckle

Scarlet Musk Flower

Scarlet musk flower, a member of the four o'clock family, is native to southwest Texas, growing in calcareous or limestone soils. The striking flowers bloom in clusters up to three inches across. Scarlet musk flower spreads horizontally with conspicuously hairy foliage. It gets its name from its offensive scent.

Native White Hibiscus

Okra

Okra

I enjoyed okra as a child on the farm. This relative of hibiscus thrives during the hottest time in the summer. The hotter the weather, the faster okra grows, even up to temperatures of 109 degrees. On hot days, I have to pick okra twice a day. Legend says that okra seeds were brought to the United States from Africa by slaves, who would tuck the seeds in their hair. This very southern vegetable has about as many ways to be cooked as shrimp. I like to grill it with sesame oil, salt, and pepper. Okra is best fresh, picked at just the right maturity.

Rudbeckia (Black-Eyed Susan, Brown-Eyed Susan)

I've grown several varieties of *Rudbeckia*. *Rudbeckia* is named after Olof Rudbeck, professor of botany at the Uppsala University in Sweden, a teacher of Linnaeus. *Rudbeckias'* bright gold color make them a standout in a summer garden. Many varieties are very durable performers, needing little care.

Ornamental Peppers

Rudbeckia

Pickerel Weed

Pickerel weed is a bog plant with striking, dense purple flowers on an upright stem. I have grown mine in a bog area. (Too small of an area, I might say. I have created a bog or wetland in my pond by creating a raised area separated by a lip covered with stones and then filling this area with soil.) Pickerel weed grows in the eastern half of the United States and is considered invasive in some areas. It is found in freshwater along shorelines and in wetlands.

Pride of Barbados
(Red Bird of Paradise)

As the name implies, Pride of Barbados is not native, but is welcomed into our Texas gardens because its brilliant plumage brightens up a summer garden when it's most needed. Plumage of red, orange, and yellow sit atop tall spikes. Long red feathery stamens curling from the center of each bloom give the flower its exotic bird-like look. Bird of paradise loves hot, sunny sites.

Rock Rose

Rock rose has been a favorite of mine ever since I found it growing natively among my Ashe juniper. Rock rose is a shrubby perennial with brilliant flowers that bloom from March through November and easily survives the Hill Country's scorching heat. This pavonia, popularly known as rock rose or rose mallow, has radiant pink blooms. Rock rose thrives in its native habitat at the edge of thickets in dappled shade. It often grows at the dripline of bushes and trees, such as Ashe juniper. Rock rose prefers well-drained, rocky, alkaline soils. Rock rose is an upright plant reaching two feet in the wild and three feet in cultivation.

Ruellias
(Mexican Petunia)

Ruellias come in all sizes, from the diminutive 'Katie' *Ruellia* to those reaching four feet tall. Many are purple, but there are also pink and white ones. The pink ones are very invasive and will show up all over the garden. *Ruellias* are very hardy with a long blooming season. Some are native to the Central Texas area. *Ruellias* tolerate both wet and dry soils, performing well in both sun and shade. I even found one growing locally that appears to prefer full shade. *Ruellias* produce seed pods that rupture when dry, spreading seeds up to three feet. Because *Ruellias* reseed easily, they make an excellent ground cover but seem to decide on their own where they want to grow. Mine have literally moved from one location to another. *Ruellias* freeze to the ground, but their hardy roots survive and come back in the spring.

Ruellias

White *Ruellias*

60

'Katie' *Ruellias*

African Blue Basil

African Blue Basil

Although I've never used African blue basil for cooking, it is one of my favorite herbs. African blue basil has also been one of the honeybees' favorites. This basil blooms pro-lifically from late spring to frost (it freezes at 28 degrees). It is a very attractive plant and is very hardy and pest-free. I've grown it at the same location for fourteen years.

American Beautyberry/ French Mulberry

American beautyberry is an attractive native understory shrub. Its main attraction is its berries in the fall. Here we see both white and red ones. The fruit is a favorite of mockingbirds, providing food from fall into the winter depending on the availability of other options. American beautyberry has long arching branches and can grow up to nine feet, as mine has.

65

Tree Senna

Tree senna is a native of South America. This senna is semi-evergreen in the Hill Country and has been short-lived in my garden thanks to a combination of freeze damage and a tendency of being blown over by wind storms. A member of the pea family, canyon senna is very showy when in full bloom and even after, when seed pods are ripening.

Tree Senna

Desert Trumpet Vine

Desert
Trumpet Vine

Desert trumpet vine arises and shines in the late summer and then through the fall until frost. Its blooms are similar to its cousins: catalpa, desert willow, and yellow bells esperanza. The pink blooms are on the tips of the vines. Blooms have characteristic markings to help guide bees and hummingbirds. This plant is in full bloom as hummingbirds migrate through the Hill Country. Its vine typically freezes to the ground in the winter but returns every year.

Esperanza

Yellow bells are a cultivated variant of our native esperanza. Yellow bells would be a larger shrub if they didn't freeze to the ground. Yellow bells bloom in the hottest season. The orange variant is great for Longhorn fans looking for orange blooms at the kickoff of football season. Yellow bells are a favorite of hummingbirds and bees.

Orange Esperanza

Yellow Bells

Fall Obedient Plant

Fall obedient plant has pink to lavender tubular flowers in a spike-like cluster along the upper part of a square stem. The name "obedient" came about because you can move an individual fresh flower back and forth on the stalk and it will stay right where you put it. This plant tolerates very wet soil; as a matter of fact, it grows in areas with standing water. It is a native habitat in the eastern half of the United States, where it grows in seasonally wet areas that dry out, hence it is also very drought tolerant as well. This plant spreads aggressively by stolons. I've had to work to contain mine.

Maximilian Sunflower

Native Americans prized Maximilian sunflower for its use as food, dye, oil, and thread. Both seeds and tubers, or rhizomes, are edible. Propagation is by seed and rhizomes. Maximilian sunflowers are native to the eastern half of the United States and Texas. This hardy perennial needs full sun and can grow in a variety of conditions, but prefers moist, clay-like soils. Maximilian sunflower's tall height makes an excellent backdrop plant. Maximilian sunflower is an important wildlife food source.

Red Blood Lily

Red blood lilies were brought to the Hill Country by German settlers. These lilies first bloom and then put on leaves after they have finished blooming. They offer a delightful surprise as they make their appearance in late summer.

Spider Lily

Perhaps one of the late summer's most magical bulbs, the spider lily pops up seemingly overnight with its colorful, exotic flowers perching atop a tall, straight stem. The bold red flowers have curved petals and showy stamens. Only after the flowers finish blooming do leaves appear to replenish the bulb. This Chinese native first came to the United States via Japan in 1854 aboard one of Commodore Perry's steam-powered ships. These bulbs are sterile and only reproduce by bulb division.

Bat Face Cuphea

This native of Mexico is a very dependable hot-summer bloomer. The bat face–shaped flowers grow on you as they take center stage in the hot season. The bat face is a perennial that freezes but survives some winters in my garden. It readily reseeds, but not all offspring are true to the parent; some have variants of shape and color. Bat face is a favorite of hummingbirds, perhaps because they encounter bat face on their travels to Mexico.

Turk's Cap

Turk's cap, a Hill Country native, is also a favorite of hummingbirds. Its unique twisted flower is closed with the stamen extending beyond the closed petals. Turk's cap is hardy, drought tolerant, and disease resistant. This flower loves either shade or sun and has a long blooming season. Turk's cap freezes to the ground most winters but returns in the spring. The marble-size fruit is edible with a mealy taste and is a favorite of squirrels and mockingbirds.

The Pond

No garden would be complete without a pond. Hill Country limestone offers the perfect material for lining the edges of the pond. My favorite water lily is the 'Panama Pacific,' which blooms most of the year and is a very attractive purple with a gold center. Darwin's law of natural selection has been in effect for the goldfish that inhabit the pond. Only the black ones usually survive, as the passing blue herons seem to be able to spot the gold ones. Frogs find the pond by themselves. A chorus of bullfrogs joins the night sounds of cicadas, owls, Chuck-will's-widow, and crickets. An owl often spends early morning atop the highest roof, perhaps waiting for a frog or some other prey. I'm fortunate to have lake water to refill the pond, as it doesn't contain chlorine. An area at the pond's edge stays wet and offers a place for plants like pickerel weed to grow (if only it were bigger). A large rock shaped like a Texas Longhorn "hook 'em" sign serves as the cornerstone for the pond. The natural balance of water plants and fish makes for a very low-maintenance environment. An orange dragonfly tops off the Longhorn theme.

Fall

The northers in mid-September bring a welcome change from the torrid heat of summer. Each succeeding norther brings the prospect of cooler weather. Migrating monarch butterflies and hummingbirds ride the winds in their southward migration. Mid-September is a peak time for migrating hummingbirds. With the northers come rains that resuscitate flowers that have struggled through the summer. A favorite in the Hill Country is the golden eye daisy, which blooms in mid-October.

A wise Hill Country gardener will anticipate the change in the weather and will start a fall vegetable garden in mid-August, so vegetables can grow before the first hard freeze. Some peppers, especially the Chinese variety, will begin their most prolific season after surviving the summer heat. On the other hand, okras shut down after temperatures drop below ninety degrees—likewise for 'Texas Star' hibiscus, a relative of okra.

In fall, berries ripen that will feed the birds throughout the winter. Yaupon, possumhaw holly, and American beautyberry are among the attractive fall berries. Native flowers like Turk's cap continue to bloom until the first hard freeze. Others, like shrimp plant, reach their prime. Texas tarragon blooms in mid-October, while its cousin, copper canyon daisy, rounds out the blooming season just before the first hard freezes.

Gayfeather

Gayfeather is one of the Hill Country's hardiest flowers. This flower's beautiful violet spikes can be seen rising from plants on the caliche banks of Hill Country roads during the hottest time of the year. The flower blooms from the top of the spike downward. The magic of high drought tolerance is pulled off because the corms on the plant have an unusual ability to retain water. On the downside, care must be taken to provide sites with very good drainage and full sun. Mine actually grow best on a slope where I don't water at all. The gayfeather is often used as a cut flower.

Mexican Bush Sage

Mexican bush sage heralds from our southern neighbor, Mexico, and shares characteristics of many Mexican perennials. It will overwinter if temperatures stay above twenty-five degrees; otherwise it freezes to the ground. Mexican bush sage propagates easily from rooted stems. Leaves are a soft green with a grayish cast and a white underside. Flowering begins in summer and continues until frost. Two types are popular in the Hill Country: one with purple flowers and one with white and purple flowers. The flowers are favorites of hummingbirds, especially hummingbirds migrating to Mexico.

I've grown both the type featuring a purple calyx with a protruding white flower and the all-purple type. The Mexican bush sage freezes to the ground each winter but recovers to bloom in late summer until frost.

Mexican Bush Sage

Argentine Rainlily

Native Grapevine

Two native grape varieties have been brought into my garden by birds. One is mustang, a very sour grape, and the other is a grape with clusters of tiny fruit. This grape, also known as fall grape, is sweet when fully ripe and has relatively large seeds. Fall grape grows well in limestone, and as such it is a candidate for providing phyloxera resistant rootstock for wine grapes. The rootstocks used throughout the wine-grape world today were originally derived from North American grapes. T.V. Munson harvested vines from South Central Texas to provide phyloxera-resistant rootstock that tolerated soils with high calcium content. Fall grape was a key grape variety for his work. However, it needed to be crossbred with other North American varieties because it did not graft well.

Shrubby Blue Sage

Shrubby blue sage is a multi-stemmed shrub that grows in the shallow, rocky, sandy, gravelly, or limestone hillsides or bushy areas in the Hill Country and south Texas. The light blue color of this sage is one of my favorites. The leaves can be dried to flavor meats and other foods.

Cosmos

Once in a while an outsider enters a Hill Country garden and stays on, either surviving the extremes of summer and winter or reseeding profusely. Cosmos is one of the latter. If you are a Texas Longhorn, an orange cosmos can be very welcome during football season. Each year, a large number of cosmos reseed to offer a majestic display of orange color.

A native of Mexico, this plant is heat and drought tolerant and extremely hardy. The attractive blooms make excellent cut flowers.

Butterfly Milkweed

Butterfly milkweed is a favorite plant for the monarch butterfly, both for its flower and as a food source for the caterpillar.

Swamp Milkweed

Like the orange milkweed, this plant attracts monarch butterflies. Swamp milkweed flowers are rose-purple and the leaves are narrower than the better-known orange milkweed. As this plant's name implies, it can be grown in extremely wet areas, including heavy clay soils.

Golden Eye

Golden eye is a native of the Texas Hill Country. Golden eye suffers through the hot dry summers and then blooms by October 15 each year. Golden eye can be seen along Hill Country roads, adding its gold color in dense stands. Its vigorous growth makes it a challenging plant for cultivation; it easily crowds out other plants. Golden eye is a favorite of honeybees.

Texas Tarragon
(Mexican Mint Marigold)

The bad news is that French tarragon grows poorly in the Hill Country's hot, humid climate. The good news is that Texas tarragon makes a reasonable substitute. Texas tarragon is a late bloomer, but not as late as its cousin, copper canyon daisy. Texas tarragon ushers in the close of the fall blooming season and signals that winter is just around the corner.

Texas tarragon grows easily in a variety of soils in full sun to partial shade. In fact, it is almost an aggressive plant, as it seeds easily. It is a low-maintenance plant with few pests or problems and can get lanky if not cut back midsummer. Texas tarragon transplants easily in the winter.

Use this herb as you would use tarragon. Texas tarragon is strong, so use sparingly—and keep in mind that Texas tarragon was even used by the Aztecs as a mild stimulant. As an herb for a Hill Country garden, Texas tarragon can't be beat. It's hardy with bright fall color and good flavor.

Mexican Mint Marigold

Hill Country Aster

Fall aster puts on a spectacular display of lavender purple daisies that are so dense that its green leaves are hardly visible. Since it loves well-drained soil, aster can be planted at the intersection of landscaping boulders. This plant deserves a home in every Hill Country garden. The migrating monarch butterflies will thank you.

Peppers

I've grown many kinds of peppers. I try to grow ones that are not readily available in local grocery stores. Two of my favorites are aji dulce #1 and orchid. Orchid was a favorite of Jean Andrews—the Pepper Lady. Variants of the orchid go by various names, such as aji flor and bishop's crown. The Chinese varieties tend to do the best in the Hill Country.

Ferns

Ferns are a natural feature in a Hill Country garden, as without prompting they will find a spot to grow in a stone wall. In the winter, warmth from the stone will help the fern survive. Several varieties of ferns have chosen my garden. I planted clover fern, but the others just showed up.

Clover fern, sometimes dubbed "Texas shamrock," is a hardy Hill Country native.

Clover fern (actually a fern) makes a great ground cover. The leaves appear in quarters, forming what looks like a four-leaf clover. If you want to convince your friends that you are the luckiest person in the world, grow this plant—just don't tell them that it's not really a clover. Not only does clover fern grow in water, but it is also a very drought-tolerant plant. In its native habitat, this fern grows in ponds and streams that dry up during the summer, so it has to survive for several months under very dry conditions. This plant has a native distribution from the Rio Grande plains to Victoria, Austin, and the edge of the Hill Country.

Holly Fern

Holly Fern

Clover Fern

Wood Fern

Sedum

Sedum is almost the perfect plant. It is drought tolerant and needs very little care. Sedum thrives in full sun in soil with good drainage. As a bonus, sedum has attractive flowers in the early fall.

Red Mountain Sage

Mountain sage is a late-season bloomer, showing its best when days shorten in the fall. It shouldn't be planted near a light that stays on at night since the light will interrupt the long nighttime darkness required to initiate blooming. I always had the best luck planting mountain sage in a partially shaded spot, away from afternoon sun. Mountain sage is native to West Texas and Mexico and is an understory plant in its native habitat.

Grey Ghost

Grey ghost is an attractive, easy-to-grow succulent that needs little care. It grows in my cactus garden without special watering. Small yellow flowers appear at the end of long stems. Like many succulents, grey ghost can be propagated by breaking off a leaf or stem and planting it.

White Mistflower

White mistflower is native in the Hill Country and has been growing on the slope below my property prior to establishing itself in the garden. This plant is found on rocky hillsides and bluffs in the southern half of the Hill Country. Mine grows in crevices on my stone walls much as it would in its natural habitat. This plant is favored by butterflies. The white to pinkish-white flowers are showy and fragrant.

White mistflower
with Cactus

125

Evergreen Sumac

Evergreen sumac is one of the Hill Country's native evergreens. Comanches collected and sun dried the leaves for smoking. The showy red fruit is important food for birds and small mammals. Evergreen sumac is a large shrub with a rounded shape. New leaves have a reddish color. Mature leaves have a maroon ring after first frost.

Evergreen Sumac

Silktassel

Spider Web

Flameleaf Sumac

Flameleaf sumac is a relatively fast-growing small tree with few pests or diseases. Flameleaf is a perfect description for this Hill Country native's orange and red autumn foliage. It is a key contributor to fall color in the Hill Country. In the fall, flameleaf sumac sports beautiful candles of showy fruit. This fruit is much prized by birds throughout the winter.

As a native, it is heat, cold, and drought tolerant. A downside to this tree is that it colonizes by sending runners out to start new plants, which can disturb the order in a garden.

Cedar Elm

Cedar elms rank in the top five or ten landscape plants for the Hill Country. Unlike other elms, they are hardy and disease resistant. As a native of the Hill Country, they are also very drought tolerant. Cedar elms flower and produce fruit in the fall. Cedar elms are one of the few native trees that can grow into vertical trees. It is a host to mistletoe, a parasite that extracts water and nutrition from the tree.

Big Tooth Maple

Spicebush

Spicebush, a Texas native, is so aromatic that even brushing against it makes you aware of its presence. Both Native Americans and early settlers used the leaves and bark to make a tea intended to cure a variety of maladies. They use the fruit as a substitute for allspice. The fruit has a high lipid content, which makes it particularly attractive to migratory birds, which have high energy demands. Spicebush leaves have a soft yellow color in the fall. I must have two male trees, because I haven't seen berries on them.

Flowering Pear

There are three reasons to own a flowering pear. First, the spectacular early flowers. Second, the gorgeous fall color. Finally, the flowering pear provides winter food for birds. There are also negative qualities in that these trees are relatively short-lived, being prone to have major branches break during storms. They are also subject to blight, and they are invasive and can outcompete native plants in some habitats.

Shrimp Plant

When most flowers are closing up shop for the winter, shrimp plant comes to life with a flower that resembles a shrimp. Shrimp plant adds cheer to a late-fall garden and blooms until there is a relatively hard freeze. It is hardy and drought tolerant.

Copper Canyon Daisy

This native relative of Texas tarragon (Mexican mint marigold) waits until the last minute in fall to cover itself with gold-orange flowers. This plant is highly aromatic, both the foliage and flowers.

Persimmon

As a child, persimmons were one of my favorite fruits. I planted the Fuyu variety in my garden. It quickly yielded a bountiful harvest—that is, as long as the racoons were kept at bay by a neighbor. The best option for harvest is to wait until the persimmons are completely ripe (a bird net is necessary). The alternative is to finish ripening the persimmons by stowing them in a box with apples that give off ethylene to ripen them. I freeze them to eat throughout the year.

Satsuma

Growing Satsuma oranges is kind of a family tradition for me. My dad had several dozen Satsuma trees on the farm where I grew up. These easy-to-peel oranges were a memorable seasonal treat. Several of my brothers and I have kept up the tradition. Since low temperatures during Hill Country winters make Satsuma cultivation a risky proposition, I chose one of the cold-hardiest Satsumas—the Owari—and planted two trees in the most protected location of my garden. Because of my bluff location, my garden is perhaps a half-zone colder than other locations in the Austin area. Some years I go to great lengths to protect the trees from cold winter days using tarps and heaters. With time, one tree has grown too big to be covered easily. The two Satsumas have survived many winters without any significant damage. In fact, they have needed very little care over the years.

Nothing does more to bring back fond childhood memories than to pluck a fruit right off the tree and eat it fresh. I have been careful to avoid transmitting any potential pests from purchased oranges to my trees, as my dad admonished me for doing so as a child.

Winter

Winter is a season that defines what is possible in a Hill Country garden. Progressively harder freezes starting in November or early December end the growing season for tender annuals and most perennials. A few perennials, like copper canyon daisy and shrimp plant, survive until a hard freeze. Some winters we have as little as a few hours of below-freezing temperatures. Despite our typically moderate winter weather, gardeners often protect their favorite plants in order to extend the growing season. Some winters, gardeners are tempted to postpone the inevitable by protecting tender plants like basil or peppers. Many vegetables can survive a fall and winter freeze, likewise for herbs, including annuals such as parsley and coriander. Some herbs, like salad burnet and sorrel, thrive in winter and mature to their most robust taste during this season.

Winter brings Hill Country gardens their most unpredictable weather patterns. A once-in-a-decade, unusually severe norther will bring temperatures to single digits, ravaging plants and reminding us that we really don't live in the tropics. Gardeners roll the dice on the survival chances for their favorite palm, cactus, or evergreen. Some scramble to protect favorite plants with covers, heat lamps, or heaters, hoping to ward off the inevitable. Each plant has its own freezing temperature: basil at 28 degrees Fahrenheit; peppers at 15 to 25 degrees; cactus at 10 to 32 degrees; rosemary at 10 degrees; copper

Little Bluestem Grass

canyon daisy at 20 degrees; shrimp plant at 20 degrees; Mexican bush sage at 25 degrees.

The first hard freeze marks an important point in the annual gardening cycle. Perennials that freeze to the ground must be cut. Cool, rainy days offer an excellent time to transplant out-of-place plants. Deciduous plants like lantanas, American beautyberry, crepe myrtle, cedar elms, and many others will easily survive transplanting. Even certain evergreens can be transplanted reliably.

The winter kill can cause a gardener to be cautious with his plant selection. But soon the memory of that harsh freeze fades, the gardener's hope returns, and with it a more ambitious planting strategy seems possible.

Winter is the time to plan next year's garden. It is the season for pruning both landscape trees and fruit trees. Fallen leaves complete the cycle for the year's compost.

Cave

My home sits on a bluff above Lake Austin. This lake is actually the Texas Colorado River dammed to form a constant-level lake. The bluff slopes were carved through millions of years of erosion by the river's waters. Since some layers of stone were harder than others, the canyon walls have areas where hard stone remained while softer stone was removed underneath. This "cave" is an example.

Sorrel

I bought three sorrel plants on a whim. After some time they proved to be rigorous growers. Leaves harvested in the wintertime can be used in salads and in making sorrel soup. I had to learn what to do with sorrel by consulting the Internet. I learned of sorrel soup and I chose a recipe from South Africa that used potatoes rather than cream. Sorrel soup is a Bastille Day tradition in France. Sorrel is best harvested in the winter in the Hill Country.

Rosemary

Rosemary is one of almost everybody's favorite herbs. Many traditions, legends, and much lore surrounds it. In the past, rosemary was considered to be too tender to grow as a perennial, but an increasing number of varieties have proved to be able to withstand Hill Country winters.

Rosemary is divided into two groups, one upright and one prostrate. I've grown both; however, the location for the prostrate variety became too shady over time. Rosemary can suffer from too little water or too much water. As an evergreen, rosemaries offer welcome green color in a Hill Country winter. Likewise, its pale blue blooms are a pleasant sight.

Like garlic, rosemary's flavor is prominent in any dish. Most cooks use the young tips of the plant. I've also used the stems of branches as skewers for barbeque. Rosemary has been used throughout recorded history. Greeks thought that rosemary stimulated the brain and aided memory. Rosemary has been recognized for its medicinal properties. Rosemary is rich in volatile oils and thought to be an anti-inflammatory, antiseptic, and antioxidant.

Yaupon Holly

Yaupon holly was very much a part of my childhood, as we used it as firewood for our wood stove. I spent many hours cutting yaupon holly to clear ranch land. Winter would bring robins that fed on the berries. Yaupon holly is native to much of the eastern US. It adapts to a wide range of soils and moisture conditions. Plants are either male or female, with only female plants putting out berries. Therefore, a male plant must be within a bee's range to fertilize the female plant. Yaupon holly's scientific name, *Ilex vomitoria*, is derived from early Europeans who witnessed Native Americans consuming large quantities of a ritual purification drink and then vomiting. This tea-like drink was steeped from toasted leaves and bark of Yaupon holly. This tea contained high levels of caffeine. Caution must be used in preparation of this tea. The mildly poisonous leaves must be roasted and fully dried before steeping. The berries are slightly toxic to humans, although holly berries provide an important food source for small mammals and many different birds.

Robins in Winter

Robins were wintertime visitors on my family's ranch and they always fascinated me as a child. We would go out at night with a flashlight and catch sleepy robins with our bare hands. Yaupon berries are a favorite treat of robins.

Possumhaw Holly

Possumhaw holly's red-orange fruit is a key ornamental feature after the foliage drops in the late fall or early winter. The berries tend to survive the winter, and while they are a good source of food for birds, they are toxic to humans. Possumhaw hollies are small multi-trunk trees nine to fifteen feet tall. They grow in part shade or full sun. Possumhaw holly is a native from east Texas to the Hill Country and tolerates a wide range of soil and moisture conditions. It also tolerates poor drainage as well as an occasional drought.

Violet Crown Sunset

Fire Pit

What Hill Country garden would be complete without a fire pit? There's no better way to pay homage to our prehistoric roots than to gather around a fire on a cold winter night. Family, good friends, and some fine wine can make for a perfect evening, especially with a full moon. A natural rock ledge deck provides the perfect setting for a fire pit. An inner ring of rocks contains the fire while the outer ring of stones provides seats far enough from the fire to be comfortable. The inner ring (approximately eight feet in diameter) is formed from stones selected to fit tightly together. The outer ring is approximately twenty feet in diameter. While a wood fire is not the energy source with the lowest carbon footprint, it does use renewable fuel.

155

Rock Squirrels

Hill Country rock squirrels are darker and
more elusive than tree squirrels. They live
in crevices between rocks. My large retaining walls make an ideal home.

Carolina Jessamine

Carolina jessamine is evergreen in the Hill Country and a favorite because it puts on a spectacular display of masses of fragrant yellow flowers in the winter. It's very hardy and disease resistant.

Winter Honeysuckle

Winter honeysuckle is a delightful shrub that extends the flowering season. Its winter flowers bring spring to the garden early and provide pollen to the bees when little else is blooming. As an evergreen in the Hill Country, this shrub has helped provide privacy to our front yard. Winter honeysuckle forms a dense, tangled shrub from six to ten feet in both height and spread—just right for a privacy screen. The flowers are not very showy but are extremely fragrant.

Four Nerve Daisy

Four nerve daisy is often seen along roadsides in the Hill Country. It grows in well-drained soils and is very drought tolerant. The flowers are yellow with three-toothed petals. The flower gets its name from the four purple veins that are on both sides of each petal. The leaves form a cluster around the base of the plant. Some of mine have bloomed throughout the winter.

Leatherleaf Mahonia

Orange Trifoliate (Bloom)

I first came to know orange trifoliate as a child when my father used this plant as a root-stock for grafting Satsuma oranges. This native of China is widely used for rootstock. However, I find it attractive as an ornamental. This deciduous plant has twisted stems with large, stout spines. Late spring blooms are popular with bees. Leaves with winged petioles and three leaflets give the plant its name. The light yellow fruit, though fragrant and citrusy, is chock-full of seeds with little pulp. The pulp is very sour with a touch of bitterness. With some experimentation, I've learned to use it in an exotic margarita. After all, once you have tried lime, prickly pear, and agarita, what's next?

Flowering Quince

Flowering quince is one of the first plants to bloom, often in late winter, sometimes so early that its blooms get nipped by a late frost. These early bloomers remind us that spring is just around the corner, giving us a nudge to ensure that we are prepared. They offer us our first-cut flowers, as we can cut errant branches and force them to bloom in a vase. I chose a white and an orange one, a fitting choice for a Texas Longhorn.

Flowering Quince

Flowering Quince

Spring

Spring is the season Hill Country gardeners live for. Wise Hill Country gardeners will have completed most of their spring planting by the time spring officially arrives. I start in the fall with plants that can overwinter, like big red sage, oxeye daisy, and bluebonnets. These plants form rosettes that hug the ground to stay warm during our winter freezes. Early bloomers like redbuds, red buckeyes, anemones, and flowering bulbs announce the arrival of spring. Spring flowers compete for the attention of pollinators. Because flowers in the Hill Country depend on spring rains, they have a very condensed blooming season, rushing to seed before the dry summer.

Bluebonnets

Texas has five state flowers, each a different species of bluebonnet. In 1901, not knowing the difference between the species, the legislature chose the Texas coastal bluebonnet as the state flower. This bluebonnet was not the Central Texas one we've come to know and love in the Hill Country. That oversight was corrected in 1971, when the legislature added two more species, including the Hill Country native, along with "any other species of bluebonnet heretofore not recorded," and designated them all as the state flower. Since 1971, two additional species have been identified, one from North Texas and one from West Texas. Of course, it is the Central Texas bluebonnet that is the delight of photographers and tourists alike in the Hill Country. The Central Texas bluebonnet, along with one other species, is exclusively native to Texas.

Fascinating tales surrounding bluebonnets have been told as far back as the time when primarily Native Americans populated the Hill Country. Images of Texas and bluebonnets are inexorably linked. Jack Maguire wrote, "the bluebonnet is to Texas what the shamrock is to Ireland, the cherry blossom is to Japan, the lily is to France, the rose to England, and the tulip to Holland."

The Texas-tough bluebonnet has adapted to a climate where some years may not have enough rainfall. A very hard coat keeps seeds viable for many years. I use a rock polishing machine to duplicate the commercial scarifying process, thereby ensuring early germination. Bluebonnets germinate in the fall and overwinter as a small rosette, then they race to grow while spring rains last.

In the spring, bees eagerly await the arrival of the first bluebonnet blooms. Pictured is an example of a fascinating pollination process. Note the white spot on the upper petal. This spot attracts the bee to pollinate. As the flower ages, this spot turns magenta. Researchers have found that bees collect many times more pollen from white spotted flowers than magenta. Note how the bee lands on the lower two petals that protect the pollen as the bee lands. The lower petals open, exposing the bright orange pollen, which will be carried to the next flower by the bee. The two side petals serve to protect the lower petal.

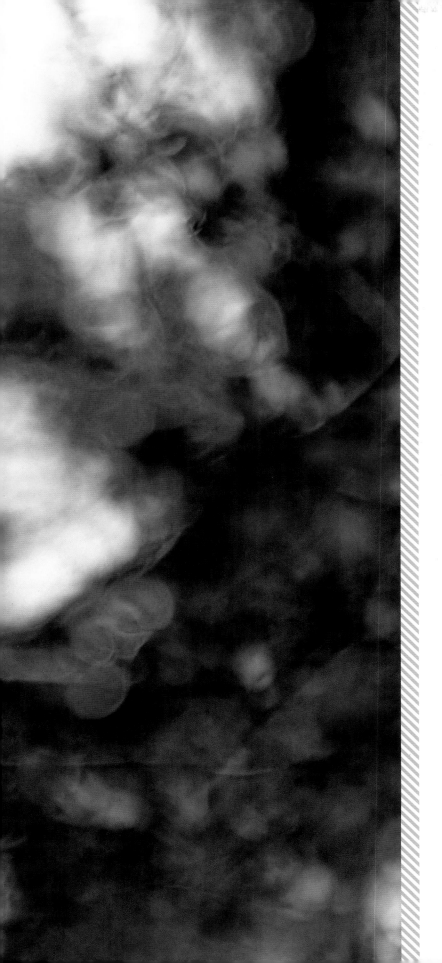

Mountain Laurel

If there is one flowering evergreen shrub that most symbolizes the Hill Country, it would be the mountain laurel. This plant has dark green foliage and tolerates thin, calcareous soils or deep, fertile soil if it's well drained. The highly aromatic purple spring blooms leave the air laden with a heavy aroma reminiscent of a just-opened grape soda pop. Both the plants and seeds are poisonous. I have grown both transplanted mountain laurels and plants from seed.

This plant is actually neither a laurel, nor is it a true mountain laurel. The Hill Country mountain laurel is a member of the legume family. The mescal bean, as this plant is sometimes known, produces woody pods that contain hard, shiny, red-orange seeds. The seeds are toxic, as they contain an alkaloid that causes convulsions and possibly even death. The narcotic qualities of these seeds were well known by Texas Native Americans. A toxic concoction made from a small amount of powder was used to induce intoxication, visions, and delirium. The shiny, hard seeds were used for necklaces and buttons.

Like the Texas bluebonnet, the Texas mountain laurel is truly unique to Texas and certainly deserves a home in any Hill Country garden.

Mountain Laurel

Redbud

One of the first signs of spring in the Hill Country is the bloom of redbud trees. The dark pink blooms can be seen across the hillsides before the foliage of other Hill Country trees such as cedar elm, flaming sumac, red oak, and shin oak emerges. To Hill Country residents, redbud blooms are an important symbol in the annual cycle of the seasons. Within weeks of the first blooms, tiny pale-green leaves appear and soon darken, taking their lovely heart-shaped form.

Agarita

Agarita is the Hill Country's member of the barberry family. It thrives on rocky slopes in well-drained loam, clay, caliche, and limestone soils. It is a slow-growing evergreen shrub that grows three to six feet tall and wide.

Agarita thrives in light shade to full sun. It is often found growing in limestone cracks. Its yellow cup-shaped flowers are some of the first to appear in spring. Agarita's pea-sized red fruit is a favorite of mockingbirds. The berries are very tasty—a welcome taste for us who like to nibble on fruit in the garden. Agarita berry juice is used to make jam or even an interesting margarita. One of the most attractive features of agaritas is their trifoliate leaf. The gray-green to blue-green leaves have three to seven lobes tipped with very sharp spines. Branches are very brittle with bright yellow wood.

Mexican Plum

Mexican plum and redbuds are two of the first ornamental trees to bloom in spring. This plant is the star of our native plums. Each spring I look forward to the dazzling array of blooms with their fragrance filling the air. Mexican plum is a beautiful single-trunked small tree with bark that eventually gets dark and striated, peeling off in patches. The early blooms offer bees their first spring feasts. The plums change color from yellow to mauve to purple as they ripen.

Scarlet Buckeye

Scarlet buckeye is a Hill Country gem. It is one of the first plants to bloom in the spring. Scarlet buckeye is special because it is so out of character in its native setting with its beautiful, delicate red bloom and its graceful leaves. The scarlet buckeye has adapted to the tough Hill Country by dropping its leaves in early August or even earlier during really dry years.

Mine has grown to only five feet in ten years. One of my favorites—I couldn't live without one. Scarlet buckeye is an understory shrub/tree in its native setting but will also grow in full sun.

Texas buckeye is a more vigorous grower and less showy than the scarlet buckeye.

Spiderwort

Spiderworts are perennials native to the Americas. At times spiderworts were considered weeds but now are considered by many to be garden treasures. Like some other natives, they tend to find their own spot in the garden. Texas has over thirty different indigenous varieties. The best choices for the Hill Country are ones native to the area. Spiderworts have clusters of three-petaled blooms ranging in color from mauve to purple. Mine bloom primarily in the spring. Spiderworts are drought tolerant and grow in a variety of soils. The wort part of the name is easy to understand, as it refers to any plant used for medicinal purposes. The spider part of the name may refer to the fact that the Cherokee used spiderwort leaves to treat spider bites.

Bulbine

Bulbines are not native to Texas, but come from South Africa. They are very hardy and drought tolerant. They require little water and care. My orange bulbines provide spring color, a nice complement to bluebonnets.

Chinese Fringe Tree

I use a Chinese fringe tree to provide screening from the street. This native of China is covered with blooms that appear as a purple fringe all over the plant. Mine is planted in an area where I intended to grow plants that required a lower pH, as this plant prefers moist, acidic soil. My plant gets morning sun but is shaded in the afternoon.

Mexican Buckeye

The name Mexican buckeye comes from the resemblance of the large brown seeds to those of the buckeye family, of which Mexican buckeye is not actually a member. Although the seeds are poisonous, they can pass through the digestive tract without causing harm. The bright pink blossoms stand out in the early spring and resemble the Texas redbud at a distance. This large branching shrub is found throughout the Hill Country in canyons and on creek banks.

Beargrass

Beargrass is a native to the Hill Country. In fact, I have a number of these indigenous beargrass plants that grow below my house. Beargrass is actually a very hardy yucca realtive and not a grass at all, able to grow in the cracks of limestone on ledges and slopes. This relative of yuccas has an attractive bloom in the springtime. Its leaves resemble that of grass, hence its name.

Scarlet Penstemon

Scarlet Penstemon

There are three penstemons native to the Hill Country. One of the showiest is scarlet penstemon. Blooms may be lavender, white, pale purple, or pink, all with purple lines inside the flower tube. Foxglove penstemon can be seen growing in open fields or along roadsides in the Hill Country. It is a very hardy perennial and readily reseeds.

Hill Country penstemon is a very eye-catching flower with long bloom stalks with numerous bright red to pinkish red tubular flowers with five lobes. The white throats of the bloom's tubes are striped with red lines. This flower grows in Hill Country canyons. Scarlet penstemon is the most beautiful penstemon native to the Hill Country. Scarlet penstemon grows in dry limestone soils of the Hill Country. The brilliant red to pinkish-red flowers are lined inside the corolla tube.

Foxglove Penstemon

Irises have gorgeous blooms and are a delight in spring gardens.

Jerusalem Sage

Jerusalem sage, a native to the Mediterranean region, is one of those non-native plants that Hill Country gardeners welcome. Striking gold-yellow flowers appear among woolly, wrinkled gray-green leaves. These evergreen plants grow in full sun and need little care. Some of mine have remained for fourteen years.

Lyre Leaf Sage

Lyre leaf sage is an edible herb native to the eastern United States. Lyre leaf sage gets its name from the shape of its leaves. This evergreen perennial makes an excellent ground cover for shady locations. In some parts of the United States, it is considered an invasive species.

Wild Onion

Just like their domesticated cousins, wild onions are edible. But beware: crow poison, a look-alike plant, is poisonous. But the onion-like smell of wild onion is the key to differentiating between the real onion and the imposter.

One type, shown on the left, has a unique approach to reproduction. In addition to flowers atop its long stems, it produces bulblets that replace individual blooms. These miniature bulbs mature and fall to the ground and grow like a bulb.

My two types of wild onions came with the soil. Wild onions can be used the same as chives in cooking.

Brazos Penstemon

Brazos penstemon has been a constant companion in my garden. This native Texas plant readily reseeds. Brazos penstemon contributed to an early theme in my garden—combinations of native and purple plants. This hardy evergreen needs little care.

Herbs

Any self-respecting gardener will have a selection of herbs in the garden. Many popular herbs will grow in a Hill Country garden. Most require good drainage and full sun for success. Herbs can be interplanted among flowers or even used as ornamentals. Cracks between large stones make an excellent spot for thyme or oregano. Some herbs, like garden sage, are short-lived in our humid climate.

Because of our heat and humidity, cultivars should be selected for their tolerance. For example, I originally selected Arp rosemary only to have it die because of heat and wetness. (Arp is one of the most cold hardy.)

Parsley has done well in the fall through spring growing seasons, going to seed in the late spring to early summer. Cilantro or coriander grows quickly and then goes to seed. Successive plantings can keep a fresh supply coming. Chives grow easily in a Hill Country garden. When I let chives seed out I end up with chives all over the garden. Basil likes full sun. I grow Italian basil for the kitchen and African basil as an ornamental.

Blue-Eyed Grass

Blue-eyed grass is actually not a grass at all but a member of the iris family. Blue-eyed grass is a short-lived perennial that likes partial sun and wet soil, even though it can grow in drier soil as well. The blossoms open for just one day in the morning and close in the afternoon. The center of the flower is gold rather than blue. This adaptable wildflower is native to open woods, meadows, and prairies of North America. Blue-eyed grass grows in clumps from rhizomes and has leaves that resemble grass.

Poppies

I've been growing the same poppies for the last fourteen years. Each year I harvest the seed to use for replanting the following year. One year I harvested over a gallon of seed. Poppies offer a big splash of color in the spring. Honeybees love them, too.

Columbine (Gold and Red)

Columbines dare us to capture their three-dimensional beauty. No matter how I try, I've come short. Perhaps when we have 3D cameras, we'll succeed.

I've grown two kinds of columbine over the years, the Hill Country native with yellow funnel-shaped petals and red spurs, and the dark yellow longspur columbine found in the Chisos mountains. The longspur is dark yellow with noticeable extended spurs. Columbines reseed easily and seem to find their favorite spot in dappled shade in well-drained soil. Columbines are early spring bloomers, blooming up to two months. Plants last three to four years, and native varieties are disease resistant.

The genus name Aquilegia is derived from the Latin for eagle (*aquila*) because of the visual connection between eagles' talons and the flower's spurs. In contrast, the name "columbine"(from the Latin *columba*) refers to doves. Viewed upside down, the flower resembles five doves nestled together. In Greek and Roman cultures, columbine was the plant of Aphrodite and Venus.

Texas Star Daisy

Texas star daisy is an annual native of the Hill Country. It is a bristly, hairy plant that starts flowering at a small height and continues from March through May. This plant is found on plains, in wooded areas, and along roadsides. Texas star daisy is easy to grow and sets just the right theme for a Lone Star garden. Even the seeds add to the star theme.

Calylophus

Calylophus is a familiar sight along Hill Country roads. Calylophus is at home among the stones in my garden. This plant's brilliant yellow flowers complement Hill Country stone very nicely. This indigenous native is extremely drought tolerant and disease resistant and will grow in the harshest conditions. I plant it at the intersection of retaining wall stones.

Western Venus looking glass is a lovely blue flower that grows on bluffs and dry hillsides. The flowers arise along a tall, erect stem.

Navajo Tea and Western Looking Glass

Navajo tea spreads by rhizomes and forms colonies on dry, calcareous outcrops throughout the Hill Country. The yellow flower heads appear atop almost leafless stems.

Cedar Sage

Cedar sage gets its name from the fact that it thrives in the dense shade of Hill Country cedars. I have cedar sage growing natively in uncultivated areas, and cedar sage in my main garden. Cedar sage is very much at home growing on limestone ledges. Cedar sage makes a delightful shady ground cover. The plant is small, about one foot tall, with leaves that are scalloped on the edges and furry on both sides. Like many spring bloomers, it winters as a rosette and then sends up several stems that bear spikes of brilliant flowers that last four to six weeks. Cedar sage is a perennial, but it also readily reseeds to help it become a dense ground cover.

Mealy Blue Sage

Mealy blue sage is named for the white felt-like, or sometimes purplish, appearance of the calyx. Mealy blue sage is a native of the Hill Country and is widespread in areas with limestone soil. Mealy blue sage is extremely hardy and is ideal for xeric gardens. This sage, like many sages, is used for medicinal purposes. The tea can be gargled or drunk for a sore throat.

Anacacho Orchid Tree

The Anacacho orchid tree can take heat, drought, and cold (to about 15 degrees Fahrenheit). This tree is covered with small blooms in the spring and attractive seedpods in the fall.

Anacua

Anacua (also called knockaway, sandpaper tree, sugar berry, or manzanita) is a small tree in the Hill Country. Anacua derives its name from the Aztec anachuita, meaning paper and tree. The name sandpaper tree is derived from the rough sandpaper texture of the leaves.

Trees growing near the lake can grow up to forty feet. The fruit, which is edible but not very tasty, is a favorite of squirrels and mockingbirds. In fact, the anacua trees in my garden were planted by birds. Anacua is semi-evergreen in Austin, shedding its leaves in hard freezes. The anacuas delivered their most prolific bounty of berries after a relatively hard freeze (13 degrees Fahrenheit) in January. Foliage is very attractive, especially new leaves after a hard freeze. In fact, anacua joins a short list of local native evergreens.

Anacua

Antelope Horn

Antelope horn milkweed derives its name from the curved shape of the seedpods. This eye-catching flower grows in a native setting below my house. Native Americans made a tea from milkweed as a tonic to strengthen the heart; the Navajo people used it as a treatment for the bite of a rabid animal. The silky down of milkweed was used in lifejackets during WWII. Antelope horn also serves as a food source for monarch caterpillars.

Barbados Cherry

Barbados cherry is a small, mostly evergreen shrub that has lovely pink and white blossoms off and on during the entire warm season. It is cold hardy to 20 degrees Fahrenheit. Its native distribution is South Texas through Mexico to South America and the Caribbean. Butterflies love the nectar, and birds quickly gobble up its bright red, edible fruit.

Blackfoot Daisy

The blackfoot daisy is a native of the Hill Country and grows in very thin caliche soil. It loves well-drained soil. I like to plant it at the intersection of retaining wall stones. Its long blooming time makes it a favorite. The blackfoot daisy gets its name from a foot-shaped bract on the rear side of the petals that turns black upon the plant's maturity.

Blue Mistflower

Blue mistflower's clusters of fuzzy blooms are a magnet for butterflies. Blue mistflower works well as a border plant or as a colonizing ground cover. It is native in the southeastern part of the United States, and is invasive in some locations. It is very hardy and needs little care.

Buffalo Grass

Buffalo grass was an important food source for buffalo throughout the Great Plains all the way from Montana to Mexico. It also is native to the Hill Country. Buffalo grass favors the Hill Country's heavy clay soils. Mine was gorgeous until the weeds and Bermuda grass came. Since then, many hours have been spent weeding.

Buffalo grass is very drought tolerant and requires careful control of moisture. Buffalo grass goes dormant during dry periods in order to survive hot, dry summers. Buffalo grass is not suitable for shady sites or areas that receive too much traffic. My lawn was sodded with 609, an all-female selection. Perhaps my choice of all-female 609 has made competing against weeds and Bermuda grass harder than it would be if the grass could reseed. One advantage to my situation: overseeding with bluebonnets is possible.

Cactus

A cactus garden would seem ideal for the Texas Hill Country; after all, most non-Texans envision the western part of our state as a dry, barren landscape with New Mexico–style cactus. In reality, a cactus garden is a somewhat tricky proposition. Most cacti require extremely well-drained soil, and high humidity can hurt many types of cactus. Each type of cactus has a specific freezing temperature.

My cactus garden soil is composed of a mixture of one-third native soil, one-third decomposed granite, and one-third sand. I would recommend a mixture that had even better drainage. A cactus garden requires full sun. Mine has become partially shaded as the live oak trees have grown.

My cactus garden has included Arizona fishhook barrel, a smaller Texas fishhook barrel, Christmas, lace from the company construction site, spineless, strawberry, Indian fig, Stetson, prickly pear, horse crippler, beavertail, and cholla.

Cacti have gorgeous blooms that last only a few days. Our local native cacti include prickly pear and lace cactus.

Christmas

Christmas

Spineless

Strawberry

Fishhook Barrel

Small Fishhook

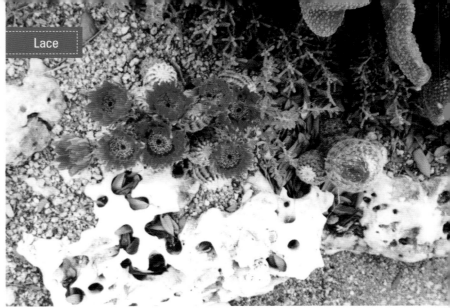

Lace

Cholla

Strawberry

Claret Cup

Claret Cup

Coral Bean

This very unique flower would be a small tree if it were not for the Hill Country freezes. My attempt to protect the trunk of this plant worked one year, but not the next. Fortunately it is root-hardy and returns in the spring, even after winters with a hard freeze. The very attractive seedpods have seeds that were used for beads by Native Americans. The seeds and all parts of the plant are poisonous. Coral bean prefers full sun but will tolerate some shade.

Coreopsis

Coreopsis's common name is "tickseed," while the name "coreopsis" means looking like an insect. Fortunately these names refer to the flattened black seed, rather than the flower. Two Texas natives, plains coreopsis (an annual) and lanceleaf (a perennial) perform well in the Hill Country. Both reseed easily.

Daylily

My aunt grew many varieties of daylilies. As a young boy I would visit her, and she would proudly show off the latest daylily variety. I planted a variety that most closely matched the burnt orange color of the Texas Longhorns. My daylilies have been hardy performers throughout the years.

Dewberry

Dewberries grow wild in much of Texas. As a child, picking and eating dewberries off the vine was always a treat. Dewberries have grown in various areas in the garden over the years. They have served as a ground cover in the rear of the house. I've picked dewberries to make dewberry cobbler. Since dewberries are more tart than blackberries, additional sugar is needed to achieve the same level of sweetness as a blackberry cobbler.

A Hill Country Forest

As a child, I would spend hours wandering around in our forestland. There's always been something special about escaping from the rest of the world. It doesn't take a very big forest to recreate the peaceful setting I experienced as a child, and although my Hill Country forest is small, I still enjoy the experience of a walk through the forest.

'Husker Red' Penstemon

'Husker Red,' a favorite in Nebraska, gets its name from the color of its leaves rather than its blooms, which are actually white to very light pink. This penstemon was introduced by Dr. Dale Lingren at the University of Nebraska.

Garden Sage

Garden sage is a popular herb that is difficult to grow in Central Texas. It requires very well-drained soil and has been short lived in my garden. Perhaps I've overwatered it, or high heat and humidity are the key villains.

Garden sage is a must for many recipes, including soups and Thanksgiving dressing. Originating from the Mediterranean, it is widely used in dishes from that area, including marinades, stews, pastas, sausages, and pâtés.

Live Oak

Live oaks are the mainstay of any Hill Country garden. Many of mine were here long before I developed my garden. I also transplanted three that were growing where my house was to be built. Because they were growing in shallow soil on solid rock, I was able to move them with a tractor front loader. I planted several that have grown rapidly. The one shown here is the centerpiece of my garden. Live oaks are very hardy and only require trimming for low-hanging branches. They renew their leaves in late winter. Live oak nuts are a major food source for squirrels and other animals.

Manfreda

Manfreda is native to the southern part of the United States from Florida to Texas. Mine has bloomed every year with tall, showy, fragrant flowers. A relative of agave, it is adapted to alkaline soils. Manfreda is a rhizomatous perennial that forms large rosettes of nearly flat, soft, fleshy sword-shaped leaves. Mine needs protection from hard freezes but has survived for many years.

Mexican Hat

Mexican hat, a Hill Country native, gets its name from its resemblance to a Mexican or ten-gallon hat. This drought-tolerant coneflower blooms through much of the summer. It thrives on neglect and is welcomed by bees and butterflies. We often take Mexican hat for granted because it is so common due to its prolific seeding habit.

Mountain Pea

Mountain pea is one of the few ground covers native to Mexico. Blue flowers add interest to this excellent evergreen. Mountain pea has proven to be hardy, surviving both our cold winters and our humid, hot summers.

Mulberry

The ranch I grew up on had several large mulberry trees. I have many fond memories of picking mulberries off the tree and eating them or saving them for a pie. Because of their short shelf life, mulberries aren't readily available in the grocery store. I have both black and white mulberries in my garden. I find the black variety much tastier than the white, plus it's much easier to tell when the black ones are ripe. I have had to remove many white mulberries planted by birds.

Native Rain Lily. Rain lilies fascinated me as a child with their habit of popping up the night after a rain.

'Nuevo Leon' Sage

'Nuevo Leon' sage is perhaps a hybrid between *Salvia greggii* (autumn sage) and *Salvia lycioides* (canyon sage). It has lovely blue-purple blooms and can be a wonderful ground cover. However, I found it not able to tolerate wet feet, as a combination of wet weather followed by hot weather caused its roots to rot. I replaced it with mountain pea with much better results.

Ocotillo

Ocotillo is a plant you would expect to see in a southwestern desert landscape. It requires a drier climate than we have in the Hill Country. As such it has only bloomed twice in my garden. It is supposed to put on leaves when it rains and then drop them and bloom. Despite the humidity, mine has survived for many years.

Oxeye Daisy

Oxeye daisy is native to Europe and was introduced to the United States as an ornamental in the 1800s. Little did we know that this beautiful flower would now be considered a noxious weed in the northwestern United States. Oxeye daisy is a hardy perennial that readily reseeds with long-lived seeds. It has been used for medicinal purposes throughout history. Our hot-dry weather prevents oxeye daisy from being an invasive species in the Hill Country.

Pink Evening Primrose

Lovely and pink, that's pink evening primrose. Its large, four-petaled flowers range in color from dark pink to white. The cup-shaped blossoms are lined with pink or red veins. In the northern part of its native range, this flower opens in the evening, true to its name. However, in the Hill Country it opens in the morning and closes in the evening. The pink evening primrose's native range was perhaps two-thirds of the central United States, possibly the same range as the American bison. Pink evening primrose is hardy and drought resistant. In my garden it has moved around as it pleases, choosing its own spot.

Prairie Verbena

Prairie Verbena

Prairie verbena is a beautiful native wildflower with light purple, round flower clusters on short stalks. Its foliage is velvety-looking, with highly divided leaves. This verbena is very drought tolerant; mine has grown in locations with no irrigation.

Purpletop Vervain

254

Purple Coneflower

The purple coneflower is a versatile flower that grows in partial shade or sun. It has a long growing season. Also known as echinacea, a well-known herb for curing the common cold, purple coneflower has been studied extensively for its immunological effects. Purple coneflower is a robust, drought-tolerant perennial and a great attractor of butterflies.

I started planting purple coneflower in the pond area because I had a request for purple flowers in that area. I also planted Brazos penstemon, purple iris, and bluebell. I learned that purple coneflower is actually more pink than purple, although a lovely color nonetheless. It does need some water to do its best. It has done well in heavy clay soils, even in relatively wet spots. Purple coneflower blooms throughout much of the year, especially if dead-headed. It also makes an outstanding, long-lasting cut flower. I propagate purple coneflower by scattering seeds wherever I want the flowers.

Purple Sage

Purple sage is sometimes called "barometer bush" because high humidity immediately after a summer rain triggers the stunning purple blooms. Purple sage is well known from Zane Gray's book *Riders of the Purple Sage*. As well as growing in the western part of the Hill Country, it can be found from northern Mexico through the Rio Grande plains and the Trans-Pecos. It grows in desert conditions, often on rocky caliche and calcareous soils.

Roses

Between high humidity and high heat, growing roses in the Hill Country can be a challenge. Fortunately for rose lovers there are some Texas stars. My favorite roses are Knock Out® and 'Belinda's Dream.' 'Belinda's Dream' was developed thanks to Dr. Robert E. Basye of Texas A&M. It is a tough rose that produces large, double pink flowers with a wonderful fragrance. It combines the toughness of an old fashioned rose with the dramatic bloom of a hybrid tea rose.

Cecile Brunner Climbing Rose

'Belinda's Dream'

Native Rose

262

Skeleton-Leaf Goldeneye

Skeleton-leaf goldeneye is a shrubby native Texas perennial. This plant has distinctively shaped leaves, hence its name. This plant tends to shade out weeds with its evergreen foliage that reaches all the way to the ground. Skeleton-leaf goldeneye is covered with daisy-like flowers from late spring to frost. This plant is drought tolerant and pest-free and requires little maintenance other than an occasional light pruning.

Spanish Lavender

Lavenders are an aromatic favorite, and will put a little of Provence, France, into your garden. In spite of being temperamental, I have been able to grow beautiful displays in my garden some years. Lavenders are susceptible to being overwatered, and I had to add special drainage on my field soil. Especially damaging is a combination of wet, rainy days followed by hot weather. Lavender is often cut and dried as an ornamental.

Stick Leaf

Stick leaf gets its name from the fact that the leaves stick tenaciously to clothing. Under high magnification, barbed hairs that look like miniature Christmas trees are visible. Once these hairs penetrate fabric, they will not come out, so be careful! Stick leaf is a semi-woody perennial that is attractive in a retaining wall.

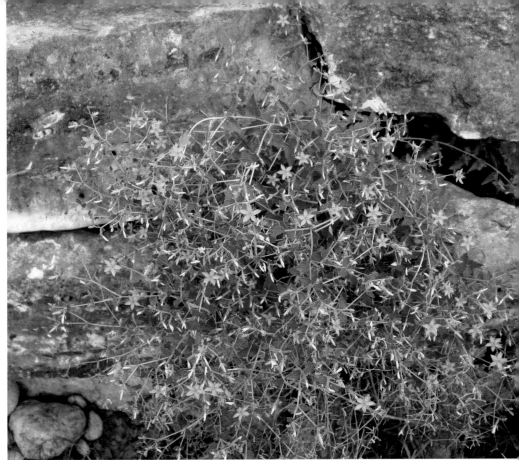

Texas Betony

Texas betony deserves a spot in every Hill Country garden. My plants have occupied the same spot for the last fourteen years. Texas betony will grow in partial shade, a real plus for this flower with its scarlet blooms. Texas betony is Texas tough. It survives droughts, poor soil, and deer and requires little water. The blooms are similar to those of the Hill Country native cedar sage.

Wine Cup (Burgundy and White)

Wine cups bring back childhood memories of a flower that could survive close grazing by cattle on our ranch. This hardy, drought-tolerant perennial is native to Texas and the central United States. Wine cups like a sunny, well-drained site. They send out multiple vine-like stems from a carrot-like central tuber. I've grown both burgundy and white wine cups. The white wine cups appear to be somewhat hardier than the burgundy ones. The two intermix, with various shades of light pink offspring. Wine cups bloom throughout the spring, die back during the hottest months of the summer, and return in the fall, staying evergreen throughout the winter. The blooms open in the morning and close at night, then close permanently after pollination.

Prairie Celestials

Pink Gaura

Twisted Leaf Yucca

Twisted leaf yucca is a hardy native of the Hill Country. It is easily identified by a noticeable twist in the leaves. The showy blooms can be seen throughout the Hill Country. The flowers are edible and were an important food source for Native Americans.

Bluebell

The Texas bluebell, a member of the gentian family, is found in moist, sunny spots throughout Texas, including the Hill Country. In fact, Blue Bell ice cream is named after these lovely flowers. Unfortunately, their desirability as a cut flower has made them scarce in the wild. However, they can still be seen along roads and spring-fed streams and rivers. Bluebells have fleshy green stems that range from one to three feet tall.

Elderberry

Elderberries have very showy white flowers and berries that are favorites of mockingbirds. My elderberries were planted by birds. Elderberry plants spread by roots, which means they can invade a flowerbed. Elderberries have been used to make wine. The berries are slightly toxic when raw but can safely be eaten when cooked. Likewise for the flowers. I had some battered and fried blooms as a dessert in Germany. Besides flowers and berries, other parts of the plant—bark, leaves, and wood—are very toxic.

Giant Coneflower

The giant coneflower is a Texas-size plant
that makes a statement in a spring garden.

Giant Sunflower/Russian Sunflower

I planted giant Russian sunflowers one season and thereafter had hybrid sunflowers that mixed with Hill Country sunflowers. These hybrids have varied in size and growth habit. The many seeds of the giant sunflower were appreciated by the birds, especially redbirds.

Hybrid Giant Sunflower

Sunflowers hybridize easily. I have had hybrids ever since I grew Russian giant sunflowers. These have varied in size from slightly larger than the native Hill Country sunflower to the size of the ones shown here. Their growing characteristics have varied as well, with some having a single bloom to multi-bloom plants.

Bog Sage

Bog sage grows up to five feet tall. Lovely sky-blue blooms top the plant's very slender stems. Bog sage is very hardy and, as its name implies, can grow in wet soil. Bog sage is cold-hardy and thrives in full sun. I cut mine back after it has bloomed in the spring to get a second bloom. Bog sage is a favorite of bees.

Indigo Spires

Indigo spires is a cultivated hybrid with lovely deep blue bloom spires. It is drought and heat tolerant and grows to a height of four to five feet. It is a favorite of bumblebees and honeybees.

Monarda

As members of the mint family, monardas share common traits with mints like aromatic scent and square stems. Monardas are ideal for Hill Country gardens. They are an important pollen source for bees and other insects, and they are very drought tolerant. Like columbines, monardas challenge the photographer to get the perfect picture, capturing the full 3D character of monarda's lovely blooms. Monardas need full sun for best results. Monardas have a long history of medicinal use by Indian tribes. The oil found in the leaves contains thymol, a chemical known for its antiseptic, antimicrobial, and antifungal properties. The name bee balm comes from monarda's use as a treatment for bee stings, skin infections, and minor wounds. Thymol is now an ingredient in many mouthwashes, following an earlier practice of using monarda teas to treat mouth and throat infections.

Purple horsemint is an indigenous annual in the Hill Country. Large colonies can be seen in fields. I planted seed to get mine started. Lighter-colored varieties with similar characteristics have appeared in my garden from time to time.

My favorite monarda is commonly called bee balm or wild bergamot. This monarda is very drought tolerant and has been a reliable performer in my garden. This perennial, while relatively short lived, has readily reseeded.

Red bergamot is an attractive perennial with a bright red flower.

Horsemint Monarda

Bee Balm Monarda

280

Red Monarda

Mountain Pink

Mountain pink grows in the harshest of caliche soils. It requires well-drained soils, often growing on caliche slopes. It adorns Hill Country roads with its beautiful bouquet of pink flowers. Mountain pinks were a favorite of Lady Bird Johnson along with its cousin, Texas centaury, or Lady Bird centaury. It has done very well in the cracks in my natural rock deck. I couldn't get enough pictures of it.

Nerve
Ray Daisy

Nerve ray is an open, bushy plant found on rocky ground, as was mine. Flowers appear as if half the petals have been plucked.

Rock Penstemon

Rock penstemon is a summer blooming perennial native of the Hill Country and western United States. With its name, rock penstemon is a natural to have growing among the stones in a Hill Country garden. In fact, this plant's native habitat is limestone crevices and bluffs of the Hill Country and beyond. Very good drainage is necessary.

Standing Cypress

Standing cypress with its feathery, light-green foliage topped with a thick, red-orange spike of flowers is a real standout in a Hill Country garden. Standing cypress's trumpet-shaped flowers are a favorite of hummingbirds. The plant is a biennial; the first year it has a basal rosette of fern-like foliage, and the second year it sends up a tall spike of flowers producing seed before dying. Standing cypress grows in both full sun and partial shade.

Yarrow

Yarrow is an attractive plant with leaves that resemble those of ferns. Yarrow is an aromatic plant with a strong but pleasant odor. It is related to chamomile and a type of wormwood from which absinthe is made.

Zexmenia

Zexmenia is an extremely hardy and drought-tolerant Hill Country native. It is a lovely local native with gold-yellow flowers. Zexmenia blooms from May to November. It prefers full sun but will grow in dappled shade. Zexmenia needs well-drained sand, loam, clay, caliche, or limestone. Zexmenia is a must for any xeriscaped Hill Country garden.

The Four-Legged Critters

One of the attractions of the Hill Country is the abundance of wildlife. The downside of having a healthy wildlife scene is that many critters view a garden as a dining room. Deer are the most challenging. They eat most anything when they are hungry. The only solution I know is a six-foot fence. A six-foot iron fence surrounds my garden—it works. Squirrels love figs, plums, and other fruit. If I wait more than a few days to pick the figs, the squirrels will devour them. Raccoons enjoy persimmons and pears. Skunks can complicate your life, especially if you have a dog. A red fox appears in my garden some evenings—but rarely during the day—from a den on the bluff. Armadillos frequent at night and once in a while in the daytime. They search for grubs and worms, leaving holes in the soil, sometimes even uprooting plants. But what Hill Country garden would be complete without armadillos?

Firewheel

Firewheel is well known to Texans because this annual is frequently seen along roadsides and in fields covering large areas. Firewheel is a hardy, drought-tolerant native to the central United States.

The Sunset

The memories linger,
ten thousand sunsets have passed.
Some splendid, some simple,
each one seems like the last.

The sun paints the sky with
its final ray
The clouds a burnt orange
any Longhorn would say.

An infinite array of colors, perhaps
a gaze on heaven's gates of gold
This one's just for you, one like it,
never again I'm told.

A tranquility like a life well-lived
as the sun goes down.
The light fades, orange and gold
turn to violet, then a violent crown.

The sky darkens, dark clouds appear,
for there's more to do.
The flowers are thirsty, the earth parched;
rain falls as if commanded to.

A parting gift perhaps, before
the clouds are swept away.
Now flowers appear, thank you
they seem to say.

The sun burns hot for summers here
now the sunset a simple orange sphere.

Acknowledgments

I would like to thank the staff at Greenleaf Book Group, especially Amber Hales, Kris Pauls, and Neil Gonzalez for their assistance in editing text and selecting photos. Damon Waitt and Joe Marcus from the Lady Bird Johnson Wildflower Center were very helpful in identifying plants.

Furthermore, I would like to thank all the horticulturists who have dedicated their lives to discovering and cultivating native Hill Country flowers. I would like to give special thanks to the Lady Bird Johnson Wildflower Center for making native plants available for research and cultivation. I would also like to thank the Native Texas Nursery, Pat McNeal, and Dan Hosage for supplying hard-to-get natives.

Finally, I would like to thank my family for their love and support in making both the garden and this book possible. We have shared many walks through the garden and wonderful evenings around the fire pit, talking about good times and enjoying the beautiful setting of the Texas Hill Country. Thank you for all the help you have given me in organizing and writing this book, which provides a record of these past fourteen years.

Index